MW00914486

not your average

GRATITUDE
JOURNAL

Not Your Average Gratitude Journal by Gratitude Daily
Published by Creative Ideas Publishing

For permissions contact:
permissions@creativeideaspublishing.com

ISBN: 978-1-952016-31-8

Hi,

The journal will help you to start each day with the right perspective. The simple layout invites you to easily practice gratitude, which is known to increase happiness. It will also make you feel more confident and balanced as you follow the prompts to organize your thoughts before the demands of the day sweep you off your feet.

Um yes, I'll take some happiness with a side of confidence and balance please!

Inside, you will find 14 "Challenge Pages;" one for each Saturday of this 100-day journey. The special pages include reflective questions intended to increase thankfulness and healthiness in various areas of your life. So, if you start this journal on a Monday, the special challenges will fall on Saturdays and the humorous quotes will fall on Wednesdays to give you a boost mid-week!

PS: Make sure to customize your own goal on the blank line in the "evening reflection" section. It can change as often as you'd like.

Enjoy the journey,

XO,
Jori Outlaw

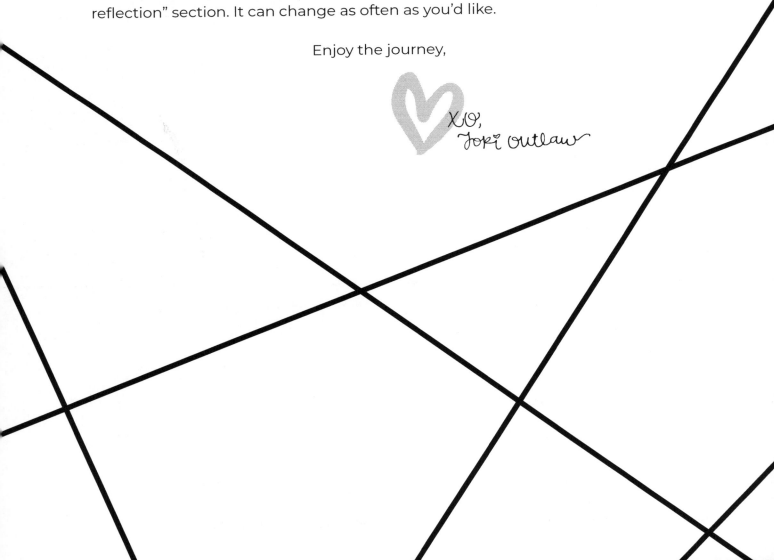

TODAY'S PRIORITIES

> " I wish retail therapy was covered by my health insurance. "

Things I'm thankful for:

1. _____
2. _____
3. _____

ONE WIN I HAD YESTERDAY WAS...

Today, I'm looking forward to:

Thoughts & Dreams

EVENING REFLECTION: Evaluate how content you are with these areas of your life today

HEALTH (CIRCLE FOR NUTRITION. MARK "X" FOR EXERCISE.) 0 1 2 3 4 5 6 7 8 9 10

OVERALL ATTITUDE TOWARDS MYSELF 0 1 2 3 4 5 6 7 8 9 10

OVERALL ATTITUDE TOWARDS OTHERS 0 1 2 3 4 5 6 7 8 9 10

_____ 0 1 2 3 4 5 6 7 8 9 10

TODAY'S PRIORITIES

> " If you want to change the future, you must change what you're doing in the present.
> -Mark Twain "

ONE WIN I HAD YESTERDAY WAS...

Things I'm thankful for:

1. _____
2. _____
3. _____

Today, I'm looking forward to:

Thoughts & Dreams

EVENING REFLECTION: Evaluate how content you are with these areas of your life today

HEALTH (CIRCLE FOR NUTRITION. MARK "X" FOR EXERCISE.)   0 1 2 3 4 5 6 7 8 9 10

OVERALL ATTITUDE TOWARDS MYSELF   0 1 2 3 4 5 6 7 8 9 10

OVERALL ATTITUDE TOWARDS OTHERS   0 1 2 3 4 5 6 7 8 9 10

_____   0 1 2 3 4 5 6 7 8 9 10

TODAY'S PRIORITIES

"
Do more of what makes you forget to look at your phone.
"

ONE WIN I HAD YESTERDAY WAS...

Things I'm thankful for:

1. _____
2. _____
3. _____

Today, I'm looking forward to:

Thoughts & Dreams

EVENING REFLECTION: Evaluate how content you are with these areas of your life today

HEALTH (CIRCLE FOR NUTRITION. MARK "X" FOR EXERCISE.) 0 1 2 3 4 5 6 7 8 9 10

OVERALL ATTITUDE TOWARDS MYSELF 0 1 2 3 4 5 6 7 8 9 10

OVERALL ATTITUDE TOWARDS OTHERS 0 1 2 3 4 5 6 7 8 9 10

_____ 0 1 2 3 4 5 6 7 8 9 10

JOT down some of the best decisions you ever made and why they were so great:

1.

2.

3.

4.

5.

TODAY'S PRIORITIES

> "No act of kindness, no matter how small, is ever wasted.
> -Aesop"

Things I'm thankful for:

1. _____
2. _____
3. _____

ONE WIN I HAD YESTERDAY WAS...

Today, I'm looking forward to:

Thoughts & Dreams

EVENING REFLECTION: Evaluate how content you are with these areas of your life today

HEALTH (CIRCLE FOR NUTRITION. MARK "X" FOR EXERCISE.) 0 1 2 3 4 5 6 7 8 9 10

OVERALL ATTITUDE TOWARDS MYSELF 0 1 2 3 4 5 6 7 8 9 10

OVERALL ATTITUDE TOWARDS OTHERS 0 1 2 3 4 5 6 7 8 9 10

_____ 0 1 2 3 4 5 6 7 8 9 10

TODAY'S PRIORITIES

> " A flower does not think of competing with the flower next to it. It just blooms.
> -Zen Shin "

ONE WIN I HAD YESTERDAY WAS...

Things I'm thankful for:

1. _____

2. _____

3. _____

Today, I'm looking forward to:

Thoughts & Dreams

EVENING REFLECTION: Evaluate how content you are with these areas of your life today

HEALTH (CIRCLE FOR NUTRITION. MARK "X" FOR EXERCISE.)　　0 1 2 3 4 5 6 7 8 9 10

OVERALL ATTITUDE TOWARDS MYSELF　　0 1 2 3 4 5 6 7 8 9 10

OVERALL ATTITUDE TOWARDS OTHERS　　0 1 2 3 4 5 6 7 8 9 10

_____　　0 1 2 3 4 5 6 7 8 9 10

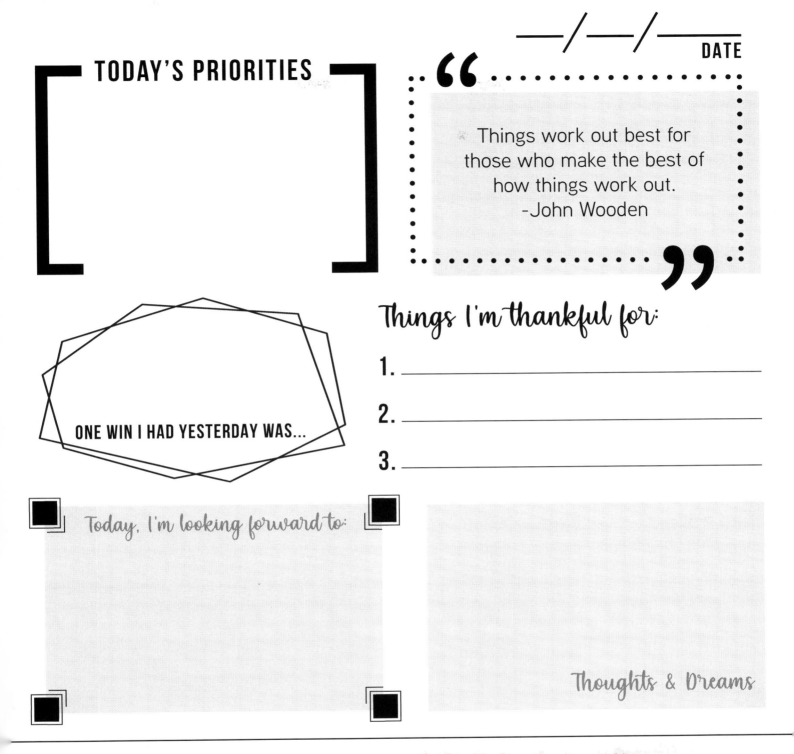

TODAY'S PRIORITIES

_____/_____/_____
DATE

" Things work out best for those who make the best of how things work out.
-John Wooden "

ONE WIN I HAD YESTERDAY WAS...

Things I'm thankful for:

1. _____
2. _____
3. _____

Today, I'm looking forward to:

Thoughts & Dreams

EVENING REFLECTION: Evaluate how content you are with these areas of your life today

HEALTH (CIRCLE FOR NUTRITION. MARK "X" FOR EXERCISE.)   0 1 2 3 4 5 6 7 8 9 10

OVERALL ATTITUDE TOWARDS MYSELF   0 1 2 3 4 5 6 7 8 9 10

OVERALL ATTITUDE TOWARDS OTHERS   0 1 2 3 4 5 6 7 8 9 10

_____   0 1 2 3 4 5 6 7 8 9 10

TODAY'S PRIORITIES

> "The first testicular guard (cup) was used in hockey in 1874 and the first helmet was used in 1974. That means it only took 100 years for men to realize that their brain is also important."

ONE WIN I HAD YESTERDAY WAS...

Things I'm thankful for:

1. _____

2. _____

3. _____

Today, I'm looking forward to:

Thoughts & Dreams

EVENING REFLECTION: Evaluate how content you are with these areas of your life today

HEALTH (CIRCLE FOR NUTRITION. MARK "X" FOR EXERCISE.)   0 1 2 3 4 5 6 7 8 9 10

OVERALL ATTITUDE TOWARDS MYSELF   0 1 2 3 4 5 6 7 8 9 10

OVERALL ATTITUDE TOWARDS OTHERS   0 1 2 3 4 5 6 7 8 9 10

_____   0 1 2 3 4 5 6 7 8 9 10

TODAY'S PRIORITIES

> "Your visions will become clear only when you can look into your own heart. Who looks outside, dreams; who looks inside, awakes.
> -Carl Jung"

ONE WIN I HAD YESTERDAY WAS...

Things I'm thankful for:

1. _____
2. _____
3. _____

Today, I'm looking forward to:

Thoughts & Dreams

EVENING REFLECTION: Evaluate how content you are with these areas of your life today

HEALTH (CIRCLE FOR NUTRITION. MARK "X" FOR EXERCISE.)   0 1 2 3 4 5 6 7 8 9 10

OVERALL ATTITUDE TOWARDS MYSELF   0 1 2 3 4 5 6 7 8 9 10

OVERALL ATTITUDE TOWARDS OTHERS   0 1 2 3 4 5 6 7 8 9 10

_____   0 1 2 3 4 5 6 7 8 9 10

TODAY'S PRIORITIES

> "We can complain because rose bushes have thorns or rejoice because thorns have roses.
> -Alphonse Karr"

Things I'm thankful for:

1. _____
2. _____
3. _____

ONE WIN I HAD YESTERDAY WAS...

Today, I'm looking forward to:

Thoughts & Dreams

EVENING REFLECTION: Evaluate how content you are with these areas of your life today

HEALTH (CIRCLE FOR NUTRITION. MARK "X" FOR EXERCISE.) 0 1 2 3 4 5 6 7 8 9 10

OVERALL ATTITUDE TOWARDS MYSELF 0 1 2 3 4 5 6 7 8 9 10

OVERALL ATTITUDE TOWARDS OTHERS 0 1 2 3 4 5 6 7 8 9 10

_____ 0 1 2 3 4 5 6 7 8 9 10

Short-Goals to Achieve Within the Year

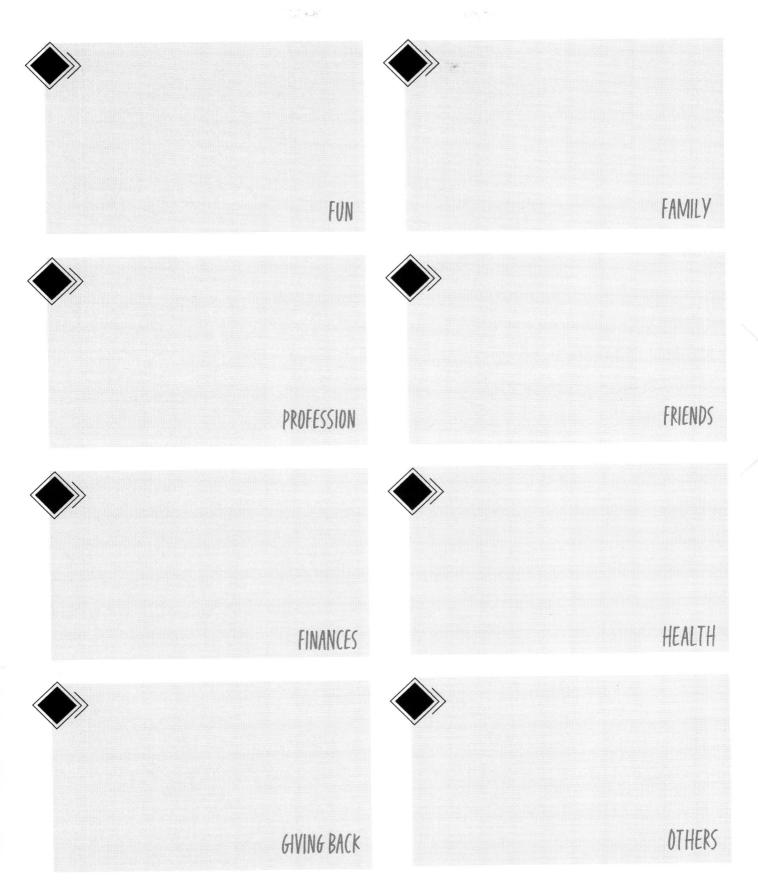

FUN

FAMILY

PROFESSION

FRIENDS

FINANCES

HEALTH

GIVING BACK

OTHERS

TODAY'S PRIORITIES

___/___/___ DATE

> "What consumes your mind controls your life."

ONE WIN I HAD YESTERDAY WAS...

Things I'm thankful for:

1. _____

2. _____

3. _____

Today, I'm looking forward to:

Thoughts & Dreams

EVENING REFLECTION: Evaluate how content you are with these areas of your life today

HEALTH (CIRCLE FOR NUTRITION. MARK "X" FOR EXERCISE.)   0 1 2 3 4 5 6 7 8 9 10

OVERALL ATTITUDE TOWARDS MYSELF   0 1 2 3 4 5 6 7 8 9 10

OVERALL ATTITUDE TOWARDS OTHERS   0 1 2 3 4 5 6 7 8 9 10

_____   0 1 2 3 4 5 6 7 8 9 10

TODAY'S PRIORITIES

> We rise by lifting others.
> -Robert Ingersoll

ONE WIN I HAD YESTERDAY WAS...

Things I'm thankful for:

1. _____
2. _____
3. _____

Today, I'm looking forward to:

Thoughts & Dreams

EVENING REFLECTION:
Evaluate how content you are with these areas of your life today

HEALTH (CIRCLE FOR NUTRITION. MARK "X" FOR EXERCISE.)   0 1 2 3 4 5 6 7 8 9 10

OVERALL ATTITUDE TOWARDS MYSELF   0 1 2 3 4 5 6 7 8 9 10

OVERALL ATTITUDE TOWARDS OTHERS   0 1 2 3 4 5 6 7 8 9 10

_____   0 1 2 3 4 5 6 7 8 9 10

TODAY'S PRIORITIES

> " No experience is wasted.
> Everything in life is happening
> to grow you up, to fill you up,
> to help you become more of
> who you were created to be.
> -Oprah Winfrey "

Things I'm thankful for:

1. _____

2. _____

3. _____

ONE WIN I HAD YESTERDAY WAS...

Today, I'm looking forward to:

Thoughts & Dreams

EVENING REFLECTION: Evaluate how content you are with these areas of your life today

HEALTH (CIRCLE FOR NUTRITION. MARK "X" FOR EXERCISE.) 0 1 2 3 4 5 6 7 8 9 10

OVERALL ATTITUDE TOWARDS MYSELF 0 1 2 3 4 5 6 7 8 9 10

OVERALL ATTITUDE TOWARDS OTHERS 0 1 2 3 4 5 6 7 8 9 10

_____ 0 1 2 3 4 5 6 7 8 9 10

TODAY'S PRIORITIES

> I want treats, cuddles, naps, & exercise. I'm basically a puppy.

ONE WIN I HAD YESTERDAY WAS...

Things I'm thankful for:

1. _____

2. _____

3. _____

Today, I'm looking forward to:

Thoughts & Dreams

EVENING REFLECTION: Evaluate how content you are with these areas of your life today

HEALTH (CIRCLE FOR NUTRITION. MARK "X" FOR EXERCISE.)   0 1 2 3 4 5 6 7 8 9 10

OVERALL ATTITUDE TOWARDS MYSELF   0 1 2 3 4 5 6 7 8 9 10

OVERALL ATTITUDE TOWARDS OTHERS   0 1 2 3 4 5 6 7 8 9 10

_____   0 1 2 3 4 5 6 7 8 9 10

TODAY'S PRIORITIES

"
Do what you can, with what you have, where you are right now.
-Theodore Roosevelt
"

ONE WIN I HAD YESTERDAY WAS...

Things I'm thankful for:

1. _____

2. _____

3. _____

Today, I'm looking forward to:

Thoughts & Dreams

EVENING REFLECTION: Evaluate how content you are with these areas of your life today

HEALTH (CIRCLE FOR NUTRITION. MARK "X" FOR EXERCISE.) 0 1 2 3 4 5 6 7 8 9 10

OVERALL ATTITUDE TOWARDS MYSELF 0 1 2 3 4 5 6 7 8 9 10

OVERALL ATTITUDE TOWARDS OTHERS 0 1 2 3 4 5 6 7 8 9 10

_____ 0 1 2 3 4 5 6 7 8 9 10

TODAY'S PRIORITIES

> " A friend is someone who understands your past, believes in your future, and accepts you just the way you are.
> -Bernard Meltzer "

Things I'm thankful for:

1. _____

2. _____

3. _____

ONE WIN I HAD YESTERDAY WAS...

Today, I'm looking forward to:

Thoughts & Dreams

EVENING REFLECTION: Evaluate how content you are with these areas of your life today

HEALTH (CIRCLE FOR NUTRITION. MARK "X" FOR EXERCISE.)   0 1 2 3 4 5 6 7 8 9 10

OVERALL ATTITUDE TOWARDS MYSELF   0 1 2 3 4 5 6 7 8 9 10

OVERALL ATTITUDE TOWARDS OTHERS   0 1 2 3 4 5 6 7 8 9 10

_____   0 1 2 3 4 5 6 7 8 9 10

FUN

FAMILY

PROFESSION

FRIENDS

FINANCES

HEALTH

GIVING BACK

OTHERS

TODODAY'S PRIORITIES

> Do not complain about growing old. It is a privilege denied to many.
> -Mark Twain

Things I'm thankful for:

1. _____
2. _____
3. _____

ONE WIN I HAD YESTERDAY WAS...

Today, I'm looking forward to:

Thoughts & Dreams

EVENING REFLECTION: Evaluate how content you are with these areas of your life today

HEALTH (CIRCLE FOR NUTRITION. MARK "X" FOR EXERCISE.) 0 1 2 3 4 5 6 7 8 9 10

OVERALL ATTITUDE TOWARDS MYSELF 0 1 2 3 4 5 6 7 8 9 10

OVERALL ATTITUDE TOWARDS OTHERS 0 1 2 3 4 5 6 7 8 9 10

_____ 0 1 2 3 4 5 6 7 8 9 10

TODAY'S PRIORITIES

> " The purpose of life is not to be happy. It is to be useful, to be honorable, to be compassionate, to have it make some difference that you have lived and lived well.
> -Ralph Waldo Emerson "

Things I'm thankful for:

1. _____
2. _____
3. _____

ONE WIN I HAD YESTERDAY WAS...

Today, I'm looking forward to:

Thoughts & Dreams

EVENING REFLECTION: Evaluate how content you are with these areas of your life today

HEALTH (CIRCLE FOR NUTRITION. MARK "X" FOR EXERCISE.)	0 1 2 3 4 5 6 7 8 9 10
OVERALL ATTITUDE TOWARDS MYSELF	0 1 2 3 4 5 6 7 8 9 10
OVERALL ATTITUDE TOWARDS OTHERS	0 1 2 3 4 5 6 7 8 9 10
_____	0 1 2 3 4 5 6 7 8 9 10

[TODAY'S PRIORITIES]

> " The grass is greener where you water it.
> -Neil Barringham "

One win I had yesterday was...

Things I'm thankful for:

1. _____

2. _____

3. _____

Today, I'm looking forward to:

Thoughts & Dreams

EVENING REFLECTION: Evaluate how content you are with these areas of your life today

HEALTH (CIRCLE FOR NUTRITION. MARK "X" FOR EXERCISE.)   0 1 2 3 4 5 6 7 8 9 10

OVERALL ATTITUDE TOWARDS MYSELF   0 1 2 3 4 5 6 7 8 9 10

OVERALL ATTITUDE TOWARDS OTHERS   0 1 2 3 4 5 6 7 8 9 10

_____   0 1 2 3 4 5 6 7 8 9 10

TODAY'S PRIORITIES

> If you were able to believe in Santa for like 8 years, you can believe in yourself for like 5 minutes.

ONE WIN I HAD YESTERDAY WAS...

Things I'm thankful for:

1. _____

2. _____

3. _____

Today, I'm looking forward to:

Thoughts & Dreams

EVENING REFLECTION: Evaluate how content you are with these areas of your life today

HEALTH (CIRCLE FOR NUTRITION. MARK "X" FOR EXERCISE.)   0 1 2 3 4 5 6 7 8 9 10

OVERALL ATTITUDE TOWARDS MYSELF   0 1 2 3 4 5 6 7 8 9 10

OVERALL ATTITUDE TOWARDS OTHERS   0 1 2 3 4 5 6 7 8 9 10

_____   0 1 2 3 4 5 6 7 8 9 10

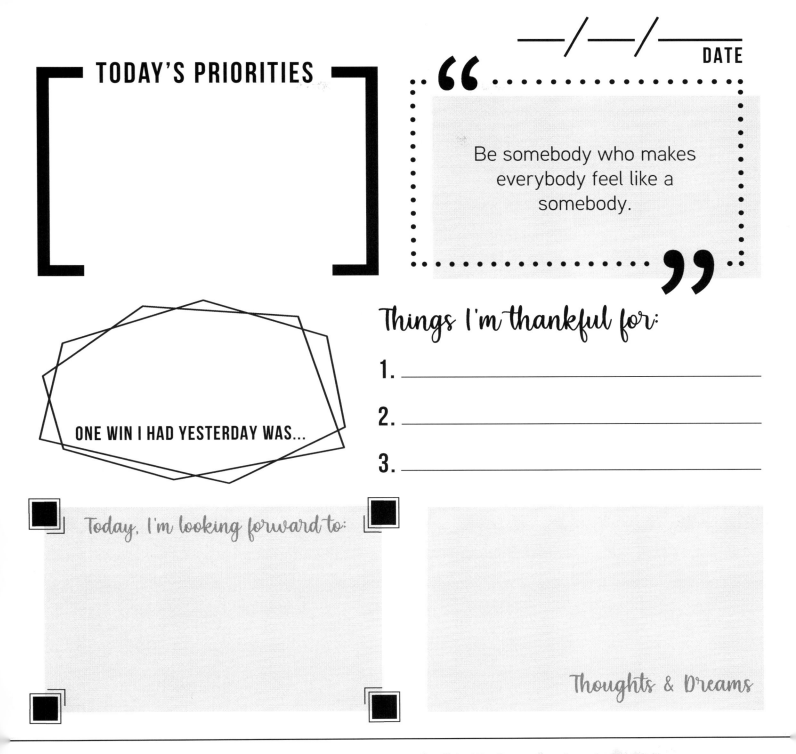

TODAY'S PRIORITIES

___/___/___ DATE

> "Be somebody who makes everybody feel like a somebody."

ONE WIN I HAD YESTERDAY WAS...

Things I'm thankful for:

1. _____

2. _____

3. _____

Today, I'm looking forward to:

Thoughts & Dreams

EVENING REFLECTION: Evaluate how content you are with these areas of your life today

HEALTH (CIRCLE FOR NUTRITION. MARK "X" FOR EXERCISE.)   0 1 2 3 4 5 6 7 8 9 10

OVERALL ATTITUDE TOWARDS MYSELF   0 1 2 3 4 5 6 7 8 9 10

OVERALL ATTITUDE TOWARDS OTHERS   0 1 2 3 4 5 6 7 8 9 10

_____   0 1 2 3 4 5 6 7 8 9 10

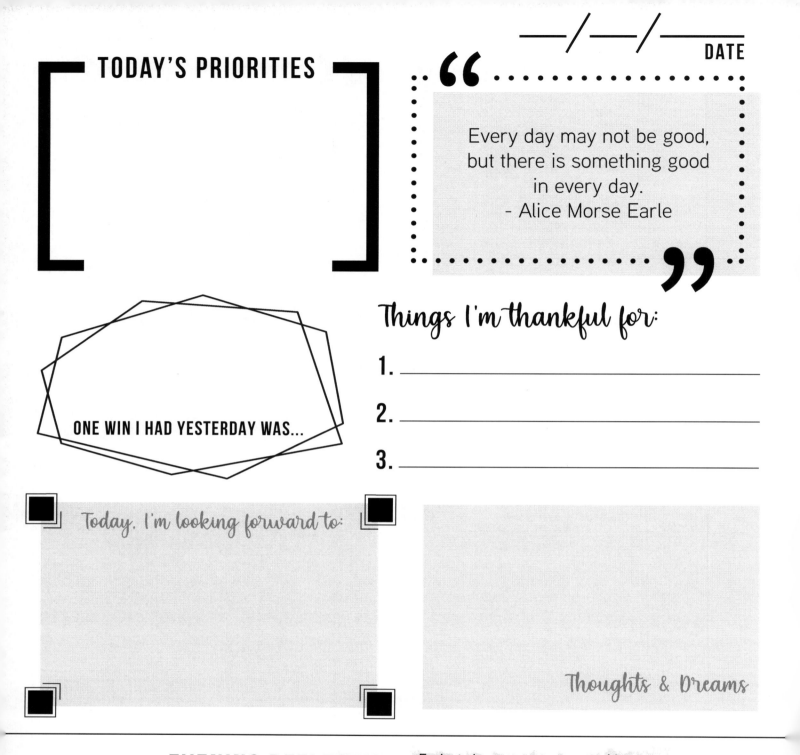

TODAY'S PRIORITIES

——/——/—— DATE

> " Every day may not be good,
> but there is something good
> in every day.
> - Alice Morse Earle "

ONE WIN I HAD YESTERDAY WAS...

Things I'm thankful for:

1. _____

2. _____

3. _____

Today, I'm looking forward to:

Thoughts & Dreams

EVENING REFLECTION: Evaluate how content you are with these areas of your life today

HEALTH (CIRCLE FOR NUTRITION. MARK "X" FOR EXERCISE.)   0 1 2 3 4 5 6 7 8 9 10

OVERALL ATTITUDE TOWARDS MYSELF   0 1 2 3 4 5 6 7 8 9 10

OVERALL ATTITUDE TOWARDS OTHERS   0 1 2 3 4 5 6 7 8 9 10

_____   0 1 2 3 4 5 6 7 8 9 10

Name something in every room of your house that you are thankful for and why:

gratitude turns what you have into enough

[TODAY'S PRIORITIES]

> "You will face many defeats in life, but never let yourself be defeated.
> -Maya Angelou"

Things I'm thankful for:

1. _____
2. _____
3. _____

ONE WIN I HAD YESTERDAY WAS...

Today, I'm looking forward to:

Thoughts & Dreams

EVENING REFLECTION: Evaluate how content you are with these areas of your life today

HEALTH (CIRCLE FOR NUTRITION. MARK "X" FOR EXERCISE.) 0 1 2 3 4 5 6 7 8 9 10

OVERALL ATTITUDE TOWARDS MYSELF 0 1 2 3 4 5 6 7 8 9 10

OVERALL ATTITUDE TOWARDS OTHERS 0 1 2 3 4 5 6 7 8 9 10

_____ 0 1 2 3 4 5 6 7 8 9 10

TODAY'S PRIORITIES

> Why should the way I feel depend on the thoughts in someone else's head?
> -Ralph Waldo Emerson

ONE WIN I HAD YESTERDAY WAS...

Things I'm thankful for:

1. _____
2. _____
3. _____

Today, I'm looking forward to:

Thoughts & Dreams

EVENING REFLECTION: Evaluate how content you are with these areas of your life today

HEALTH (CIRCLE FOR NUTRITION. MARK "X" FOR EXERCISE.)　0 1 2 3 4 5 6 7 8 9 10

OVERALL ATTITUDE TOWARDS MYSELF　0 1 2 3 4 5 6 7 8 9 10

OVERALL ATTITUDE TOWARDS OTHERS　0 1 2 3 4 5 6 7 8 9 10

_____　0 1 2 3 4 5 6 7 8 9 10

TODAY'S PRIORITIES

> " If you look at what you have in life, you'll always have more. If you look at what you don't have in life, you'll never have enough.
> -Oprah Winfrey "

ONE WIN I HAD YESTERDAY WAS...

Things I'm thankful for:

1. _____
2. _____
3. _____

Today, I'm looking forward to:

Thoughts & Dreams

EVENING REFLECTION: Evaluate how content you are with these areas of your life today

HEALTH (CIRCLE FOR NUTRITION. MARK "X" FOR EXERCISE.)　0 1 2 3 4 5 6 7 8 9 10

OVERALL ATTITUDE TOWARDS MYSELF　0 1 2 3 4 5 6 7 8 9 10

OVERALL ATTITUDE TOWARDS OTHERS　0 1 2 3 4 5 6 7 8 9 10

_____　0 1 2 3 4 5 6 7 8 9 10

TODAY'S PRIORITIES

> My favorite exercise is a cross between a lunge and a crunch... I call it lunch.

ONE WIN I HAD YESTERDAY WAS...

Things I'm thankful for:

1. _____
2. _____
3. _____

Today, I'm looking forward to:

Thoughts & Dreams

EVENING REFLECTION: Evaluate how content you are with these areas of your life today

HEALTH (CIRCLE FOR NUTRITION. MARK "X" FOR EXERCISE.)   0 1 2 3 4 5 6 7 8 9 10

OVERALL ATTITUDE TOWARDS MYSELF   0 1 2 3 4 5 6 7 8 9 10

OVERALL ATTITUDE TOWARDS OTHERS   0 1 2 3 4 5 6 7 8 9 10

_____   0 1 2 3 4 5 6 7 8 9 10

TODAY'S PRIORITIES

"
In three words I can sum up everything I've learned about life: it goes on.
-Robert Frost
"

Things I'm thankful for:

1. _____

2. _____

3. _____

ONE WIN I HAD YESTERDAY WAS...

Today, I'm looking forward to:

Thoughts & Dreams

EVENING REFLECTION: Evaluate how content you are with these areas of your life today

HEALTH (CIRCLE FOR NUTRITION. MARK "X" FOR EXERCISE.)   0 1 2 3 4 5 6 7 8 9 10

OVERALL ATTITUDE TOWARDS MYSELF   0 1 2 3 4 5 6 7 8 9 10

OVERALL ATTITUDE TOWARDS OTHERS   0 1 2 3 4 5 6 7 8 9 10

_____   0 1 2 3 4 5 6 7 8 9 10

[TODAY'S PRIORITIES]

" Do not let making a living prevent you from making a life.
-John Wooden "

ONE WIN I HAD YESTERDAY WAS...

Things I'm thankful for:

1. _____
2. _____
3. _____

Today, I'm looking forward to:

Thoughts & Dreams

EVENING REFLECTION: Evaluate how content you are with these areas of your life today

HEALTH (CIRCLE FOR NUTRITION. MARK "X" FOR EXERCISE.) 0 1 2 3 4 5 6 7 8 9 10

OVERALL ATTITUDE TOWARDS MYSELF 0 1 2 3 4 5 6 7 8 9 10

OVERALL ATTITUDE TOWARDS OTHERS 0 1 2 3 4 5 6 7 8 9 10

_____ 0 1 2 3 4 5 6 7 8 9 10

Know Your Tribe. Love Them Hard.

NAME A FEW PEOPLE WHO
LOVE AND SUPPORT YOU...

_____

_____

_____

_____

HOW DO THEY LOVE AND SUPPORT YOU?

NAME A FEW PEOPLE WHO
INSPIRE YOU...

_____

_____

_____

_____

WHY DO THEY INSPIRE YOU?

NAME A FEW PEOPLE WHO
HAVE HELPED SHAPE YOU...

_____

_____

_____

_____

HOW DID THEY SHAPE YOU?

CONSIDER REACHING OUT TO THESE PEOPLE TO THANK AND ENCOURAGE THEM.

[TODAY'S PRIORITIES

> " Only a life lived for others
> is a life worthwhile.
> -Albert Einstein "

ONE WIN I HAD YESTERDAY WAS...

Things I'm thankful for:

1. _____
2. _____
3. _____

Today, I'm looking forward to:

Thoughts & Dreams

EVENING REFLECTION: Evaluate how content you are with these areas of your life today

HEALTH (CIRCLE FOR NUTRITION. MARK "X" FOR EXERCISE.) 0 1 2 3 4 5 6 7 8 9 10

OVERALL ATTITUDE TOWARDS MYSELF 0 1 2 3 4 5 6 7 8 9 10

OVERALL ATTITUDE TOWARDS OTHERS 0 1 2 3 4 5 6 7 8 9 10

_____ 0 1 2 3 4 5 6 7 8 9 10

TODAY'S PRIORITIES

> "Never let the fear of striking out keep you from playing the game.
> -Babe Ruth"

ONE WIN I HAD YESTERDAY WAS...

Things I'm thankful for:

1. _____
2. _____
3. _____

Today, I'm looking forward to:

Thoughts & Dreams

EVENING REFLECTION: Evaluate how content you are with these areas of your life today

HEALTH (CIRCLE FOR NUTRITION. MARK "X" FOR EXERCISE.)   0 1 2 3 4 5 6 7 8 9 10

OVERALL ATTITUDE TOWARDS MYSELF   0 1 2 3 4 5 6 7 8 9 10

OVERALL ATTITUDE TOWARDS OTHERS   0 1 2 3 4 5 6 7 8 9 10

_____   0 1 2 3 4 5 6 7 8 9 10

TODAY'S PRIORITIES

"

Mistakes are proof that you're trying.

"

ONE WIN I HAD YESTERDAY WAS...

Things I'm thankful for:

1. _____

2. _____

3. _____

Today, I'm looking forward to:

Thoughts & Dreams

EVENING REFLECTION: Evaluate how content you are with these areas of your life today

HEALTH (CIRCLE FOR NUTRITION. MARK "X" FOR EXERCISE.) 0 1 2 3 4 5 6 7 8 9 10

OVERALL ATTITUDE TOWARDS MYSELF 0 1 2 3 4 5 6 7 8 9 10

OVERALL ATTITUDE TOWARDS OTHERS 0 1 2 3 4 5 6 7 8 9 10

_____ 0 1 2 3 4 5 6 7 8 9 10

TODAY'S PRIORITIES

[ ]

> They say the best things take time... that's why I'm always late.

Things I'm thankful for:

1. _____
2. _____
3. _____

ONE WIN I HAD YESTERDAY WAS...

Today, I'm looking forward to:

Thoughts & Dreams

EVENING REFLECTION: Evaluate how content you are with these areas of your life today

HEALTH (CIRCLE FOR NUTRITION. MARK "X" FOR EXERCISE.)   0 1 2 3 4 5 6 7 8 9 10

OVERALL ATTITUDE TOWARDS MYSELF   0 1 2 3 4 5 6 7 8 9 10

OVERALL ATTITUDE TOWARDS OTHERS   0 1 2 3 4 5 6 7 8 9 10

_____   0 1 2 3 4 5 6 7 8 9 10

TODAY'S PRIORITIES

> " Surround yourself with only people who are going to lift you higher.
> -Oprah Winfrey "

Things I'm thankful for:

1. _____

2. _____

3. _____

ONE WIN I HAD YESTERDAY WAS...

Today, I'm looking forward to:

Thoughts & Dreams

EVENING REFLECTION: Evaluate how content you are with these areas of your life today

HEALTH (CIRCLE FOR NUTRITION. MARK "X" FOR EXERCISE.)   0 1 2 3 4 5 6 7 8 9 10

OVERALL ATTITUDE TOWARDS MYSELF   0 1 2 3 4 5 6 7 8 9 10

OVERALL ATTITUDE TOWARDS OTHERS   0 1 2 3 4 5 6 7 8 9 10

_____   0 1 2 3 4 5 6 7 8 9 10

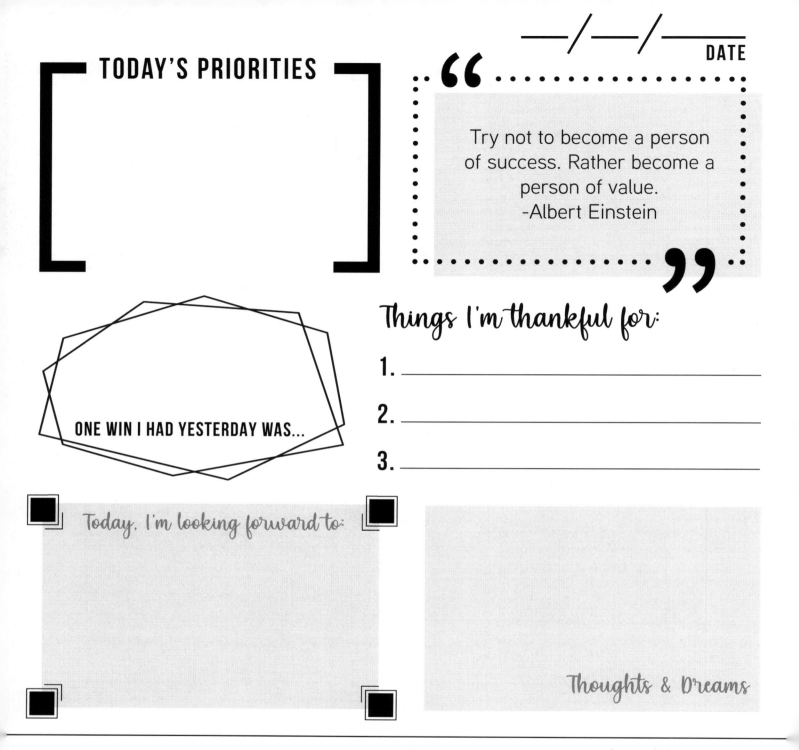

TODAY'S PRIORITIES

> Try not to become a person of success. Rather become a person of value.
> -Albert Einstein

Things I'm thankful for:

1. _____

2. _____

3. _____

ONE WIN I HAD YESTERDAY WAS...

Today, I'm looking forward to:

Thoughts & Dreams

EVENING REFLECTION: Evaluate how content you are with these areas of your life today

HEALTH (CIRCLE FOR NUTRITION. MARK "X" FOR EXERCISE.)   0 1 2 3 4 5 6 7 8 9 10

OVERALL ATTITUDE TOWARDS MYSELF   0 1 2 3 4 5 6 7 8 9 10

OVERALL ATTITUDE TOWARDS OTHERS   0 1 2 3 4 5 6 7 8 9 10

_____   0 1 2 3 4 5 6 7 8 9 10

Women can often name many things they wish they could change about their body. We frequently forget that our bodies are tools for living, not mere trophies.

List **TWENTY** things you are thankful that your body allows you to do!

1.

2.

3.

4.

5.

6.

7.

8.

9.

10.

11.

12.

13.

14.

15.

16.

17.

18.

19.

20.

Consider reaching out to a trusted person or counselor if you struggle harming your body in any way. (Ex: undereating, overeating, obsessing, self-harm, etc.)

TODAY'S PRIORITIES

> "I alone cannot change the world, but I can cast a stone across the water to create many ripples.
> -Mother Teresa"

ONE WIN I HAD YESTERDAY WAS...

Things I'm thankful for:

1. _____
2. _____
3. _____

Today, I'm looking forward to:

Thoughts & Dreams

EVENING REFLECTION: Evaluate how content you are with these areas of your life today

HEALTH (CIRCLE FOR NUTRITION. MARK "X" FOR EXERCISE.)   0 1 2 3 4 5 6 7 8 9 10

OVERALL ATTITUDE TOWARDS MYSELF   0 1 2 3 4 5 6 7 8 9 10

OVERALL ATTITUDE TOWARDS OTHERS   0 1 2 3 4 5 6 7 8 9 10

_____   0 1 2 3 4 5 6 7 8 9 10

[TODAY'S PRIORITIES]

> *The harder the conflict, the more glorious the triumph.*
> -Thomas Paine

Things I'm thankful for:

1. _____
2. _____
3. _____

ONE WIN I HAD YESTERDAY WAS...

Today, I'm looking forward to:

Thoughts & Dreams

EVENING REFLECTION: Evaluate how content you are with these areas of your life today

HEALTH (CIRCLE FOR NUTRITION. MARK "X" FOR EXERCISE.)   0 1 2 3 4 5 6 7 8 9 10

OVERALL ATTITUDE TOWARDS MYSELF   0 1 2 3 4 5 6 7 8 9 10

OVERALL ATTITUDE TOWARDS OTHERS   0 1 2 3 4 5 6 7 8 9 10

_____   0 1 2 3 4 5 6 7 8 9 10

TODAY'S PRIORITIES

> " Sometimes you will never know the value of a moment until it becomes a memory.
> -Dr. Seuss "

Things I'm thankful for:

1. _____
2. _____
3. _____

ONE WIN I HAD YESTERDAY WAS...

Today, I'm looking forward to:

Thoughts & Dreams

EVENING REFLECTION: Evaluate how content you are with these areas of your life today

HEALTH (CIRCLE FOR NUTRITION. MARK "X" FOR EXERCISE.)   0 1 2 3 4 5 6 7 8 9 10

OVERALL ATTITUDE TOWARDS MYSELF   0 1 2 3 4 5 6 7 8 9 10

OVERALL ATTITUDE TOWARDS OTHERS   0 1 2 3 4 5 6 7 8 9 10

_____   0 1 2 3 4 5 6 7 8 9 10

TODAY'S PRIORITIES

> " Me: I need some help around here! Also me: No, not like that. Here, I'll do it. "

Things I'm thankful for:

1. _____
2. _____
3. _____

ONE WIN I HAD YESTERDAY WAS...

Today, I'm looking forward to:

Thoughts & Dreams

EVENING REFLECTION: Evaluate how content you are with these areas of your life today

HEALTH (CIRCLE FOR NUTRITION. MARK "X" FOR EXERCISE.)   0 1 2 3 4 5 6 7 8 9 10

OVERALL ATTITUDE TOWARDS MYSELF   0 1 2 3 4 5 6 7 8 9 10

OVERALL ATTITUDE TOWARDS OTHERS   0 1 2 3 4 5 6 7 8 9 10

_____   0 1 2 3 4 5 6 7 8 9 10

TODAY'S PRIORITIES

> Bloom where you're planted.

Things I'm thankful for:

1. _____
2. _____
3. _____

ONE WIN I HAD YESTERDAY WAS...

Today, I'm looking forward to:

Thoughts & Dreams

EVENING REFLECTION: Evaluate how content you are with these areas of your life today

HEALTH (CIRCLE FOR NUTRITION. MARK "X" FOR EXERCISE.)   0 1 2 3 4 5 6 7 8 9 10

OVERALL ATTITUDE TOWARDS MYSELF   0 1 2 3 4 5 6 7 8 9 10

OVERALL ATTITUDE TOWARDS OTHERS   0 1 2 3 4 5 6 7 8 9 10

_____   0 1 2 3 4 5 6 7 8 9 10

TODAY'S PRIORITIES

> "You can't go back and change the beginning, but you can start where you are and change the ending.
> -C.S. Lewis"

Things I'm thankful for:

1. _____
2. _____
3. _____

ONE WIN I HAD YESTERDAY WAS...

Today, I'm looking forward to:

Thoughts & Dreams

EVENING REFLECTION: Evaluate how content you are with these areas of your life today

HEALTH (CIRCLE FOR NUTRITION. MARK "X" FOR EXERCISE.)   0 1 2 3 4 5 6 7 8 9 10

OVERALL ATTITUDE TOWARDS MYSELF   0 1 2 3 4 5 6 7 8 9 10

OVERALL ATTITUDE TOWARDS OTHERS   0 1 2 3 4 5 6 7 8 9 10

_____   0 1 2 3 4 5 6 7 8 9 10

PHYSICAL HEALTH

Evaluate the following questions on a scale of 1 through 10 with 1 being the absolute worst and 10 being the absolute best.

How healthy is my nutrition? (Let's consider this question in terms of nutrients provided to the body, not counting calories.)

1   2   3   4   5   6   7   8   9   10

Some healthy foods I enjoy are:

I'm thankful for:

Thoughts/Goals:

The USDA recommends eating 5-9 servings of fruit and veggies per day, how many am I eating?

1   2   3   4   5   6   7   8   9   10

I'm thankful for:

Thoughts/Goals:

How healthy is my strength and fitness?

1   2   3   4   5   6   7   8   9   10

I'm thankful for:

Thoughts/Goals:

How healthy is my body image?

1   2   3   4   5   6   7   8   9   10

I'm thankful for:

Thoughts/Goals:

How healthy is my hydration?

1   2   3   4   5   6   7   8   9   10

I'm thankful for:

Thoughts/Goals:

How well am I doing with the preventative medical care? (I.E. doctor check-ups, dental cleanings, eye visits, etc.)

1   2   3   4   5   6   7   8   9   10

I'm thankful for:

Thoughts/Goals:

Exercise is a celebration of what your body can do. Not a punishment for what you ate.

Health is not about the weight you lose. It's about the life you gain.

Food is fuel. Food is medicine.

[TODAY'S PRIORITIES]

> "If everything was perfect, you would never learn and you would never grow.
> -Beyoncé"

ONE WIN I HAD YESTERDAY WAS...

Things I'm thankful for:

1. _____
2. _____
3. _____

Today, I'm looking forward to:

Thoughts & Dreams

EVENING REFLECTION: Evaluate how content you are with these areas of your life today

HEALTH (CIRCLE FOR NUTRITION. MARK "X" FOR EXERCISE.)   0 1 2 3 4 5 6 7 8 9 10

OVERALL ATTITUDE TOWARDS MYSELF   0 1 2 3 4 5 6 7 8 9 10

OVERALL ATTITUDE TOWARDS OTHERS   0 1 2 3 4 5 6 7 8 9 10

_____   0 1 2 3 4 5 6 7 8 9 10

TODAY'S PRIORITIES

—/—/—
DATE

> " The more grateful I am, the more beauty I see.
> -Mary Davis "

Things I'm thankful for:

1. _____

2. _____

3. _____

ONE WIN I HAD YESTERDAY WAS...

Today, I'm looking forward to:

Thoughts & Dreams

EVENING REFLECTION: Evaluate how content you are with these areas of your life today

HEALTH (CIRCLE FOR NUTRITION. MARK "X" FOR EXERCISE.)   0 1 2 3 4 5 6 7 8 9 10

OVERALL ATTITUDE TOWARDS MYSELF   0 1 2 3 4 5 6 7 8 9 10

OVERALL ATTITUDE TOWARDS OTHERS   0 1 2 3 4 5 6 7 8 9 10

_____   0 1 2 3 4 5 6 7 8 9 10

TODAY'S PRIORITIES

"
Be so completely yourself that everyone else feels safe to be themselves too.
"

ONE WIN I HAD YESTERDAY WAS...

Things I'm thankful for:

1. _____

2. _____

3. _____

Today, I'm looking forward to:

Thoughts & Dreams

EVENING REFLECTION: Evaluate how content you are with these areas of your life today

HEALTH (CIRCLE FOR NUTRITION. MARK "X" FOR EXERCISE.) 0 1 2 3 4 5 6 7 8 9 10

OVERALL ATTITUDE TOWARDS MYSELF 0 1 2 3 4 5 6 7 8 9 10

OVERALL ATTITUDE TOWARDS OTHERS 0 1 2 3 4 5 6 7 8 9 10

_____ 0 1 2 3 4 5 6 7 8 9 10

TODAY'S PRIORITIES

> "There are two types of people:
>
> Inbox: 0
> Inbox 56,924 "

ONE WIN I HAD YESTERDAY WAS...

Things I'm thankful for:

1. _____

2. _____

3. _____

Today, I'm looking forward to:

Thoughts & Dreams

EVENING REFLECTION: Evaluate how content you are with these areas of your life today

HEALTH (CIRCLE FOR NUTRITION. MARK "X" FOR EXERCISE.)	0 1 2 3 4 5 6 7 8 9 10
OVERALL ATTITUDE TOWARDS MYSELF	0 1 2 3 4 5 6 7 8 9 10
OVERALL ATTITUDE TOWARDS OTHERS	0 1 2 3 4 5 6 7 8 9 10
_____	0 1 2 3 4 5 6 7 8 9 10

TODAY'S PRIORITIES

> Every day is a gift that's why it is called the present.

Things I'm thankful for:

1. _____

2. _____

3. _____

ONE WIN I HAD YESTERDAY WAS...

Today, I'm looking forward to:

Thoughts & Dreams

EVENING REFLECTION: Evaluate how content you are with these areas of your life today

HEALTH (CIRCLE FOR NUTRITION. MARK "X" FOR EXERCISE.)   0 1 2 3 4 5 6 7 8 9 10

OVERALL ATTITUDE TOWARDS MYSELF   0 1 2 3 4 5 6 7 8 9 10

OVERALL ATTITUDE TOWARDS OTHERS   0 1 2 3 4 5 6 7 8 9 10

_____   0 1 2 3 4 5 6 7 8 9 10

[TODAY'S PRIORITIES]

> " It is not the length of life, but depth of life.
> -Ralph Waldo Emerson "

ONE WIN I HAD YESTERDAY WAS...

Things I'm thankful for:

1. _____

2. _____

3. _____

Today. I'm looking forward to:

Thoughts & Dreams

EVENING REFLECTION: Evaluate how content you are with these areas of your life today

HEALTH (CIRCLE FOR NUTRITION. MARK "X" FOR EXERCISE.)   0 1 2 3 4 5 6 7 8 9 10

OVERALL ATTITUDE TOWARDS MYSELF   0 1 2 3 4 5 6 7 8 9 10

OVERALL ATTITUDE TOWARDS OTHERS   0 1 2 3 4 5 6 7 8 9 10

_____   0 1 2 3 4 5 6 7 8 9 10

FINANCIAL HEALTH

"You must gain control over your money or the lack of it will forever control you." – Dave Ramsey

5 TIPS TO IMPROVE YOUR FINANCIAL HEALTH:

1. Spend less than you earn. This is way easier said than done, but nowadays inexpensive websites and apps (i.e. YNAB, EveryDollar) can help tremendously by providing easy-to-use budgets that even sync with your bank account. The word "budget" can make people tighten up with all sorts of negative emotions, but it's actually a tool for freedom. Poor financial health affects stress, relationships, lifestyle, and more. Budgeting simply helps you know where every dollar of your money is going.

2. Attack debt. Debt is easily acquired through student loans, car payments, store credit cards, and many other avenues. It oftentimes starts off with hope to pay loans off quickly, but then interest rates are tacked on and more loans get added that take you further than you planned to go and hinder your life. The first step is simple: Stop taking on any kind of new debt. The second step is to prioritize paying off any current debt. For more support in this pursuit, research Dave Ramsey's "Debt Snowball Method."

3. Set up an emergency fund. "78 percent of U.S. workers live paycheck to paycheck to make ends meet," Careerbuilder discovered. This means there is no money going into savings to help when unforeseen hardships happen. Emergency funds ideally have three to six months (or more) of your income saved to cover such unexpected expenses. Pro tip: It's helpful to separate this fund from your checking account so that it's less tempting to spend.

4. Make financial goals. Jot down a few goals you may have such as a holiday vacation, house down payment, saving or investing. Then look at your income and expenses and figure out how to achieve your goals. It may take trimming certain expenses or taking on a side hustle, but if you keep your eyes fixed on why you're sacrificing, you are more likely to make it happen.

5. Learn about investment. Investing can seem intimidating, but it can be easily learned or guided, and it offers many benefits, most noteworthy being retirement. A great first step is to listen to an informative podcast, read an article or book, or set up a free advice call with a financial planner.

RECOMMENDED FINANCIAL RESOURCES:

• Dave Ramsey has resources across all platforms from podcasts to online articles to books and more. A great first purchase would be his best-selling book "The Total Money Makeover: A Proven Plan for Financial Fitness".

• Clark Howard, Suze Orman, and Rachel Cruze all have popular resources and tips out as well on money management.

• Etsy.com has many "financial planner printables" if you find yourself needing inexpensive and customizable tools for financial freedom journey.

REFLECTIVE QUESTIONS:

Do you tend to be a saver or a spender? What are some advantages and disadvantages to your answer?

What person, book, or podcast has ever taught you about good money management?

What are a few steps you could take to improve your financial health?

_____/_____/_____ **DATE**

[TODAY'S PRIORITIES]

> " Enjoy the little things, for one day you may look back and realize they were the big things.
> -Robert Brault "

ONE WIN I HAD YESTERDAY WAS...

Things I'm thankful for:

1. _____

2. _____

3. _____

Today, I'm looking forward to:

Thoughts & Dreams

EVENING REFLECTION: Evaluate how content you are with these areas of your life today

HEALTH (CIRCLE FOR NUTRITION. MARK "X" FOR EXERCISE.)   0 1 2 3 4 5 6 7 8 9 10

OVERALL ATTITUDE TOWARDS MYSELF   0 1 2 3 4 5 6 7 8 9 10

OVERALL ATTITUDE TOWARDS OTHERS   0 1 2 3 4 5 6 7 8 9 10

_____   0 1 2 3 4 5 6 7 8 9 10

[TODAY'S PRIORITIES]

> "When we seek to discover the best in others, we somehow bring out the best in ourselves.
> -William Arthur Ward "

ONE WIN I HAD YESTERDAY WAS...

Things I'm thankful for:

1. _____

2. _____

3. _____

Today, I'm looking forward to:

Thoughts & Dreams

EVENING REFLECTION: Evaluate how content you are with these areas of your life today

HEALTH (CIRCLE FOR NUTRITION. MARK "X" FOR EXERCISE.)   0 1 2 3 4 5 6 7 8 9 10

OVERALL ATTITUDE TOWARDS MYSELF   0 1 2 3 4 5 6 7 8 9 10

OVERALL ATTITUDE TOWARDS OTHERS   0 1 2 3 4 5 6 7 8 9 10

_____   0 1 2 3 4 5 6 7 8 9 10

TODAY'S PRIORITIES

" Small steps in the right direction can turn out to be the biggest step of your life. "

Things I'm thankful for:

1. _____
2. _____
3. _____

ONE WIN I HAD YESTERDAY WAS...

Today, I'm looking forward to:

Thoughts & Dreams

EVENING REFLECTION: Evaluate how content you are with these areas of your life today

HEALTH (CIRCLE FOR NUTRITION. MARK "X" FOR EXERCISE.)   0 1 2 3 4 5 6 7 8 9 10

OVERALL ATTITUDE TOWARDS MYSELF   0 1 2 3 4 5 6 7 8 9 10

OVERALL ATTITUDE TOWARDS OTHERS   0 1 2 3 4 5 6 7 8 9 10

_____   0 1 2 3 4 5 6 7 8 9 10

TODAY'S PRIORITIES

> Raising kids is a walk in the park... Jurassic park.

Things I'm thankful for:

1. _____

2. _____

3. _____

ONE WIN I HAD YESTERDAY WAS...

Today, I'm looking forward to:

Thoughts & Dreams

EVENING REFLECTION: Evaluate how content you are with these areas of your life today

HEALTH (CIRCLE FOR NUTRITION. MARK "X" FOR EXERCISE.)   0 1 2 3 4 5 6 7 8 9 10

OVERALL ATTITUDE TOWARDS MYSELF   0 1 2 3 4 5 6 7 8 9 10

OVERALL ATTITUDE TOWARDS OTHERS   0 1 2 3 4 5 6 7 8 9 10

_____   0 1 2 3 4 5 6 7 8 9 10

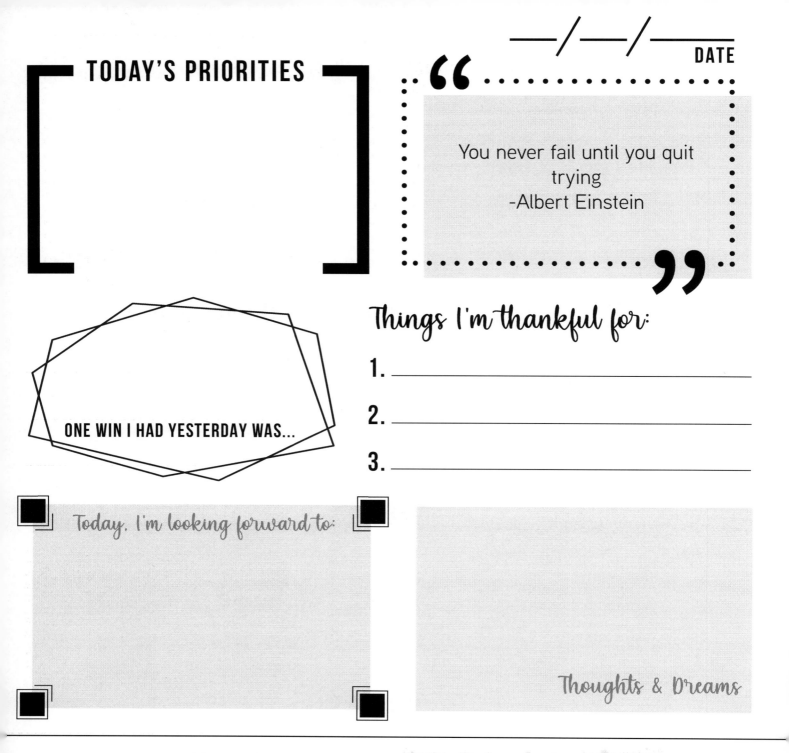

[TODAY'S PRIORITIES]

——/——/——
DATE

" You never fail until you quit trying
-Albert Einstein "

Things I'm thankful for:

1. _____

2. _____

3. _____

ONE WIN I HAD YESTERDAY WAS...

Today, I'm looking forward to:

Thoughts & Dreams

EVENING REFLECTION: Evaluate how content you are with these areas of your life today

HEALTH (CIRCLE FOR NUTRITION. MARK "X" FOR EXERCISE.)   0 1 2 3 4 5 6 7 8 9 10

OVERALL ATTITUDE TOWARDS MYSELF   0 1 2 3 4 5 6 7 8 9 10

OVERALL ATTITUDE TOWARDS OTHERS   0 1 2 3 4 5 6 7 8 9 10

_____   0 1 2 3 4 5 6 7 8 9 10

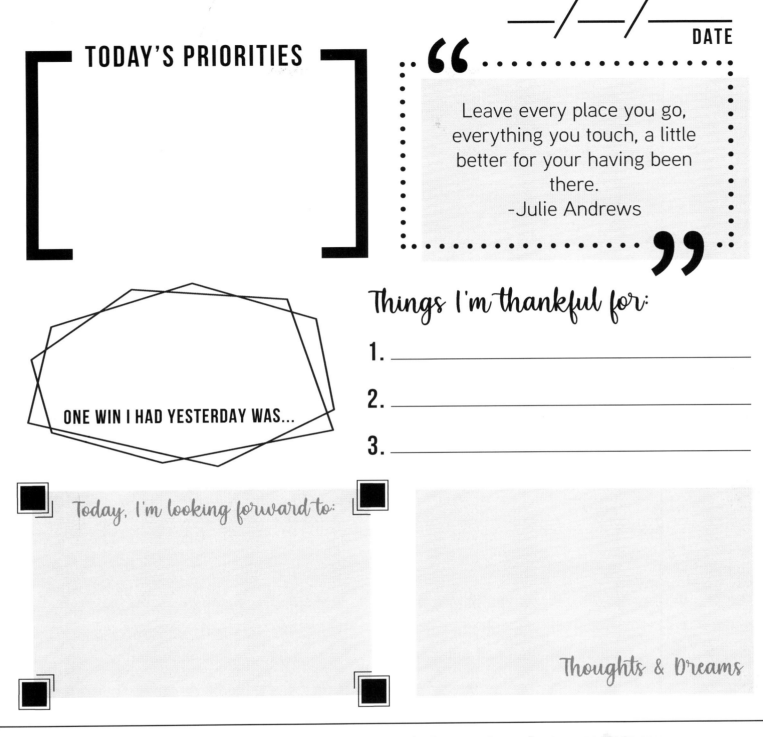

TODAY'S PRIORITIES

> " Leave every place you go, everything you touch, a little better for your having been there.
> -Julie Andrews "

Things I'm thankful for:

1. _____
2. _____
3. _____

ONE WIN I HAD YESTERDAY WAS...

Today, I'm looking forward to:

Thoughts & Dreams

EVENING REFLECTION: Evaluate how content you are with these areas of your life today

HEALTH (CIRCLE FOR NUTRITION. MARK "X" FOR EXERCISE.)   0 1 2 3 4 5 6 7 8 9 10

OVERALL ATTITUDE TOWARDS MYSELF   0 1 2 3 4 5 6 7 8 9 10

OVERALL ATTITUDE TOWARDS OTHERS   0 1 2 3 4 5 6 7 8 9 10

_____   0 1 2 3 4 5 6 7 8 9 10

MENTAL HEALTH

What are 5 things that stir up positivity in you?

1.

2.

3.

4.

5.

we fall.
we break.
WE FAIL.
but
then,
WE RISE.
we heal.
WE OVERCOME.

1. What are some things in your life that tend to cause negativity in you?

2. Are there any steps you could take towards elimination of those things?

3. What are some habits that might could improve your mental health?
(e.g., daily walks outside, 5-minute deep breathing exercises, counseling, healthy boundaries in commitments, screen time, etc.)

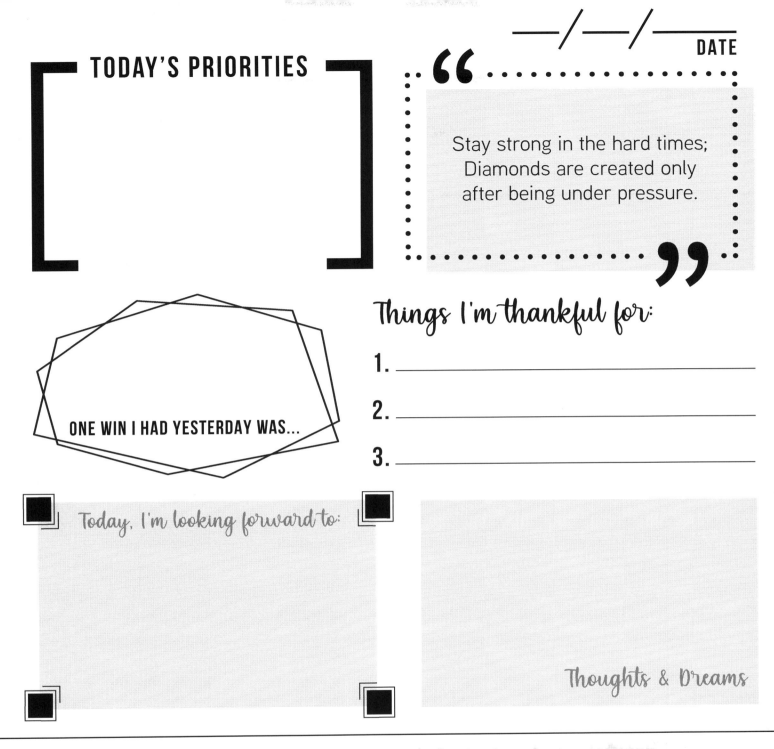

TODAY'S PRIORITIES

_____/_____/_____
DATE

" Stay strong in the hard times; Diamonds are created only after being under pressure. "

ONE WIN I HAD YESTERDAY WAS...

Things I'm thankful for:

1. _____

2. _____

3. _____

Today, I'm looking forward to:

Thoughts & Dreams

EVENING REFLECTION: Evaluate how content you are with these areas of your life today

HEALTH (CIRCLE FOR NUTRITION. MARK "X" FOR EXERCISE.)   0 1 2 3 4 5 6 7 8 9 10

OVERALL ATTITUDE TOWARDS MYSELF   0 1 2 3 4 5 6 7 8 9 10

OVERALL ATTITUDE TOWARDS OTHERS   0 1 2 3 4 5 6 7 8 9 10

_____   0 1 2 3 4 5 6 7 8 9 10

TODAY'S PRIORITIES

—/—/—
DATE

> " Some people come in our life as blessings. Some come in your life as lessons.
> -Mother Teresa "

ONE WIN I HAD YESTERDAY WAS...

Things I'm thankful for:

1. _____

2. _____

3. _____

Today, I'm looking forward to:

Thoughts & Dreams

EVENING REFLECTION: Evaluate how content you are with these areas of your life today

HEALTH (CIRCLE FOR NUTRITION. MARK "X" FOR EXERCISE.)   0 1 2 3 4 5 6 7 8 9 10

OVERALL ATTITUDE TOWARDS MYSELF   0 1 2 3 4 5 6 7 8 9 10

OVERALL ATTITUDE TOWARDS OTHERS   0 1 2 3 4 5 6 7 8 9 10

_____   0 1 2 3 4 5 6 7 8 9 10

TODAY'S PRIORITIES

> " Accept both compliments and criticism. It takes both sun and rain for a flower to grow. "

ONE WIN I HAD YESTERDAY WAS...

Things I'm thankful for:

1. _____
2. _____
3. _____

Today, I'm looking forward to:

Thoughts & Dreams

EVENING REFLECTION: Evaluate how content you are with these areas of your life today

HEALTH (CIRCLE FOR NUTRITION. MARK "X" FOR EXERCISE.)   0 1 2 3 4 5 6 7 8 9 10

OVERALL ATTITUDE TOWARDS MYSELF   0 1 2 3 4 5 6 7 8 9 10

OVERALL ATTITUDE TOWARDS OTHERS   0 1 2 3 4 5 6 7 8 9 10

_____   0 1 2 3 4 5 6 7 8 9 10

TODAY'S PRIORITIES

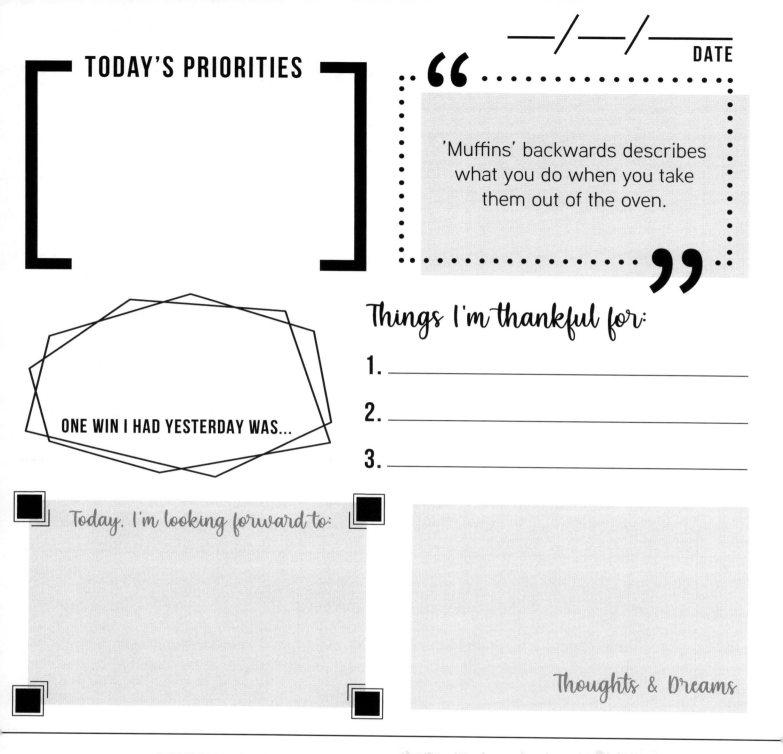

---/---/___
DATE

> 'Muffins' backwards describes what you do when you take them out of the oven.

Things I'm thankful for:

1. _____

2. _____

3. _____

ONE WIN I HAD YESTERDAY WAS...

Today, I'm looking forward to:

Thoughts & Dreams

EVENING REFLECTION: Evaluate how content you are with these areas of your life today

HEALTH (CIRCLE FOR NUTRITION. MARK "X" FOR EXERCISE.)   0 1 2 3 4 5 6 7 8 9 10

OVERALL ATTITUDE TOWARDS MYSELF   0 1 2 3 4 5 6 7 8 9 10

OVERALL ATTITUDE TOWARDS OTHERS   0 1 2 3 4 5 6 7 8 9 10

_____   0 1 2 3 4 5 6 7 8 9 10

TODAY'S PRIORITIES

" *She saw every ending as a new beginning.* "

Things I'm thankful for:

1. _____

2. _____

3. _____

ONE WIN I HAD YESTERDAY WAS...

Today, I'm looking forward to:

Thoughts & Dreams

EVENING REFLECTION: Evaluate how content you are with these areas of your life today

HEALTH (CIRCLE FOR NUTRITION. MARK "X" FOR EXERCISE.)	0 1 2 3 4 5 6 7 8 9 10
OVERALL ATTITUDE TOWARDS MYSELF	0 1 2 3 4 5 6 7 8 9 10
OVERALL ATTITUDE TOWARDS OTHERS	0 1 2 3 4 5 6 7 8 9 10
_____	0 1 2 3 4 5 6 7 8 9 10

TODAY'S PRIORITIES

> "Don't go through life, Grow through life.
> -Eric Butterworth"

Things I'm thankful for:

1. _____
2. _____
3. _____

ONE WIN I HAD YESTERDAY WAS...

Today, I'm looking forward to:

Thoughts & Dreams

EVENING REFLECTION: Evaluate how content you are with these areas of your life today

HEALTH (CIRCLE FOR NUTRITION. MARK "X" FOR EXERCISE.) 0 1 2 3 4 5 6 7 8 9 10

OVERALL ATTITUDE TOWARDS MYSELF 0 1 2 3 4 5 6 7 8 9 10

OVERALL ATTITUDE TOWARDS OTHERS 0 1 2 3 4 5 6 7 8 9 10

_____ 0 1 2 3 4 5 6 7 8 9 10

"No experience is wasted. Everything in life is happening to grow you up, to fill you up, to help you become more of who you were created to be."

• • • •

Oprah Winfrey

Write about a time or two when good came from a hard situation.

TODAY'S PRIORITIES

> " Strong women don't put others down… They lift them up.
> -Michael P Watson "

ONE WIN I HAD YESTERDAY WAS...

Things I'm thankful for:

1. _____
2. _____
3. _____

Today, I'm looking forward to:

Thoughts & Dreams

EVENING REFLECTION: Evaluate how content you are with these areas of your life today

HEALTH (CIRCLE FOR NUTRITION. MARK "X" FOR EXERCISE.) 0 1 2 3 4 5 6 7 8 9 10

OVERALL ATTITUDE TOWARDS MYSELF 0 1 2 3 4 5 6 7 8 9 10

OVERALL ATTITUDE TOWARDS OTHERS 0 1 2 3 4 5 6 7 8 9 10

_____ 0 1 2 3 4 5 6 7 8 9 10

TODAY'S PRIORITIES

> "There are friends. There is family. And then there are friends that become family."

ONE WIN I HAD YESTERDAY WAS...

Things I'm thankful for:

1. _____

2. _____

3. _____

Today, I'm looking forward to:

Thoughts & Dreams

EVENING REFLECTION: Evaluate how content you are with these areas of your life today

HEALTH (CIRCLE FOR NUTRITION. MARK "X" FOR EXERCISE.)   0 1 2 3 4 5 6 7 8 9 10

OVERALL ATTITUDE TOWARDS MYSELF   0 1 2 3 4 5 6 7 8 9 10

OVERALL ATTITUDE TOWARDS OTHERS   0 1 2 3 4 5 6 7 8 9 10

_____   0 1 2 3 4 5 6 7 8 9 10

TODAY'S PRIORITIES

> " When you can't control what's happening, challenge yourself to control the way you respond to what's happening. That's where your power is. "

Things I'm thankful for:

1. _____

2. _____

3. _____

ONE WIN I HAD YESTERDAY WAS...

Today, I'm looking forward to:

Thoughts & Dreams

EVENING REFLECTION: Evaluate how content you are with these areas of your life today

HEALTH (CIRCLE FOR NUTRITION. MARK "X" FOR EXERCISE.) 0 1 2 3 4 5 6 7 8 9 10

OVERALL ATTITUDE TOWARDS MYSELF 0 1 2 3 4 5 6 7 8 9 10

OVERALL ATTITUDE TOWARDS OTHERS 0 1 2 3 4 5 6 7 8 9 10

_____ 0 1 2 3 4 5 6 7 8 9 10

TODAY'S PRIORITIES

> " This evening, I plan to be as useless as the 'g' in 'lasagna'. "

Things I'm thankful for:

1. _____

2. _____

3. _____

ONE WIN I HAD YESTERDAY WAS...

Today, I'm looking forward to:

Thoughts & Dreams

EVENING REFLECTION: Evaluate how content you are with these areas of your life today

HEALTH (CIRCLE FOR NUTRITION. MARK "X" FOR EXERCISE.) 0 1 2 3 4 5 6 7 8 9 10

OVERALL ATTITUDE TOWARDS MYSELF 0 1 2 3 4 5 6 7 8 9 10

OVERALL ATTITUDE TOWARDS OTHERS 0 1 2 3 4 5 6 7 8 9 10

_____ 0 1 2 3 4 5 6 7 8 9 10

TODAY'S PRIORITIES

" Be mindful of the future...
but not at the expense of
the moment.
-Qui Gon Jinn "

ONE WIN I HAD YESTERDAY WAS...

Things I'm thankful for:

1. _____
2. _____
3. _____

Today, I'm looking forward to:

Thoughts & Dreams

EVENING REFLECTION:
Evaluate how content you are with these areas of your life today

HEALTH (CIRCLE FOR NUTRITION. MARK "X" FOR EXERCISE.)   0 1 2 3 4 5 6 7 8 9 10

OVERALL ATTITUDE TOWARDS MYSELF   0 1 2 3 4 5 6 7 8 9 10

OVERALL ATTITUDE TOWARDS OTHERS   0 1 2 3 4 5 6 7 8 9 10

_____   0 1 2 3 4 5 6 7 8 9 10

TODAY'S PRIORITIES

> "Darkness cannot drive out darkness; only light can do that. Hate cannot drive out hate; only love can do that.
> -Martin Luther King Jr."

Things I'm thankful for:

1. _____
2. _____
3. _____

ONE WIN I HAD YESTERDAY WAS...

Today, I'm looking forward to:

Thoughts & Dreams

EVENING REFLECTION: Evaluate how content you are with these areas of your life today

HEALTH (CIRCLE FOR NUTRITION. MARK "X" FOR EXERCISE.)   0 1 2 3 4 5 6 7 8 9 10

OVERALL ATTITUDE TOWARDS MYSELF   0 1 2 3 4 5 6 7 8 9 10

OVERALL ATTITUDE TOWARDS OTHERS   0 1 2 3 4 5 6 7 8 9 10

_____   0 1 2 3 4 5 6 7 8 9 10

What book has had a positive impact on your life? How so?

What movie has had a positive impact on your life? How so?

What song(s) impacted you positively? How so?

Write about a scent that takes you back to a happy memory?

What are two things that make you happy to see?

TODAY'S PRIORITIES

> " If you don't stand for something you will fall for anything.
> -Malcolm X "

ONE WIN I HAD YESTERDAY WAS...

Things I'm thankful for:

1. _____
2. _____
3. _____

Today, I'm looking forward to:

Thoughts & Dreams

EVENING REFLECTION: Evaluate how content you are with these areas of your life today

HEALTH (CIRCLE FOR NUTRITION. MARK "X" FOR EXERCISE.) 0 1 2 3 4 5 6 7 8 9 10

OVERALL ATTITUDE TOWARDS MYSELF 0 1 2 3 4 5 6 7 8 9 10

OVERALL ATTITUDE TOWARDS OTHERS 0 1 2 3 4 5 6 7 8 9 10

_____ 0 1 2 3 4 5 6 7 8 9 10

TODAY'S PRIORITIES

> " Being positive doesn't mean you have to be happy all the time. It means that even on hard days you know that there are better ones coming. "

ONE WIN I HAD YESTERDAY WAS...

Things I'm thankful for:

1. _____
2. _____
3. _____

Today, I'm looking forward to:

Thoughts & Dreams

EVENING REFLECTION: Evaluate how content you are with these areas of your life today

HEALTH (CIRCLE FOR NUTRITION. MARK "X" FOR EXERCISE.)   0 1 2 3 4 5 6 7 8 9 10

OVERALL ATTITUDE TOWARDS MYSELF   0 1 2 3 4 5 6 7 8 9 10

OVERALL ATTITUDE TOWARDS OTHERS   0 1 2 3 4 5 6 7 8 9 10

_____   0 1 2 3 4 5 6 7 8 9 10

TODAY'S PRIORITIES

> "Failure is not fun. It can be awful. But living so cautiously that you never fail is worse.
> -J. K. Rowling"

ONE WIN I HAD YESTERDAY WAS...

Things I'm thankful for:

1. _____
2. _____
3. _____

Today, I'm looking forward to:

Thoughts & Dreams

EVENING REFLECTION: Evaluate how content you are with these areas of your life today

HEALTH (CIRCLE FOR NUTRITION. MARK "X" FOR EXERCISE.) 0 1 2 3 4 5 6 7 8 9 10

OVERALL ATTITUDE TOWARDS MYSELF 0 1 2 3 4 5 6 7 8 9 10

OVERALL ATTITUDE TOWARDS OTHERS 0 1 2 3 4 5 6 7 8 9 10

_____ 0 1 2 3 4 5 6 7 8 9 10

TODAY'S PRIORITIES

———/———/———
DATE

> " I swear I have it together. I just forgot where I put it. "

ONE WIN I HAD YESTERDAY WAS...

Things I'm thankful for:

1. _____

2. _____

3. _____

Today, I'm looking forward to:

Thoughts & Dreams

EVENING REFLECTION: Evaluate how content you are with these areas of your life today

HEALTH (CIRCLE FOR NUTRITION. MARK "X" FOR EXERCISE.)   0 1 2 3 4 5 6 7 8 9 10

OVERALL ATTITUDE TOWARDS MYSELF   0 1 2 3 4 5 6 7 8 9 10

OVERALL ATTITUDE TOWARDS OTHERS   0 1 2 3 4 5 6 7 8 9 10

_____   0 1 2 3 4 5 6 7 8 9 10

TODAY'S PRIORITIES

> Speak in such a way that others love to listen to you. Listen in such a way that others love to speak to you.
> -Zig Ziglar

Things I'm thankful for:

1. _____

2. _____

3. _____

ONE WIN I HAD YESTERDAY WAS...

Today, I'm looking forward to:

Thoughts & Dreams

EVENING REFLECTION:
Evaluate how content you are with these areas of your life today

HEALTH (CIRCLE FOR NUTRITION. MARK "X" FOR EXERCISE.)   0 1 2 3 4 5 6 7 8 9 10

OVERALL ATTITUDE TOWARDS MYSELF   0 1 2 3 4 5 6 7 8 9 10

OVERALL ATTITUDE TOWARDS OTHERS   0 1 2 3 4 5 6 7 8 9 10

_____   0 1 2 3 4 5 6 7 8 9 10

TODAY'S PRIORITIES

> Life doesn't have to be perfect to be wonderful.
> -Annette Funicello

ONE WIN I HAD YESTERDAY WAS...

Things I'm thankful for:

1. _____

2. _____

3. _____

Today. I'm looking forward to:

Thoughts & Dreams

EVENING REFLECTION: Evaluate how content you are with these areas of your life today

HEALTH (CIRCLE FOR NUTRITION. MARK "X" FOR EXERCISE.)   0 1 2 3 4 5 6 7 8 9 10

OVERALL ATTITUDE TOWARDS MYSELF   0 1 2 3 4 5 6 7 8 9 10

OVERALL ATTITUDE TOWARDS OTHERS   0 1 2 3 4 5 6 7 8 9 10

_____   0 1 2 3 4 5 6 7 8 9 10

How are you different from 5 years ago?

Reflect on some areas you have grown in.
Consider things you have learned, people you
have met, and habits or hobbies you have started or stopped.

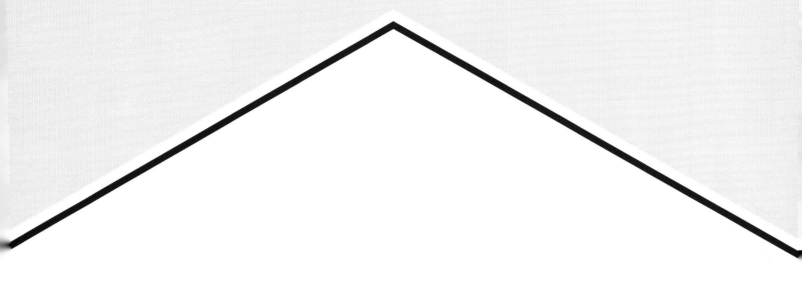

TODAY'S PRIORITIES

> "If you want to go fast,
> go alone.
>
> If you want to go far,
> go together."

ONE WIN I HAD YESTERDAY WAS...

Things I'm thankful for:

1. _____

2. _____

3. _____

Today. I'm looking forward to:

Thoughts & Dreams

EVENING REFLECTION: Evaluate how content you are with these areas of your life today

HEALTH (CIRCLE FOR NUTRITION. MARK "X" FOR EXERCISE.)   0 1 2 3 4 5 6 7 8 9 10

OVERALL ATTITUDE TOWARDS MYSELF   0 1 2 3 4 5 6 7 8 9 10

OVERALL ATTITUDE TOWARDS OTHERS   0 1 2 3 4 5 6 7 8 9 10

_____   0 1 2 3 4 5 6 7 8 9 10

TODAY'S PRIORITIES

> " We're all so busy chasing the extraordinary that we forget to stop and be grateful for the ordinary.
> -Brené Brown "

Things I'm thankful for:

1. _____

2. _____

3. _____

ONE WIN I HAD YESTERDAY WAS...

Today, I'm looking forward to:

Thoughts & Dreams

EVENING REFLECTION:
Evaluate how content you are with these areas of your life today

HEALTH (CIRCLE FOR NUTRITION. MARK "X" FOR EXERCISE.)   0 1 2 3 4 5 6 7 8 9 10

OVERALL ATTITUDE TOWARDS MYSELF   0 1 2 3 4 5 6 7 8 9 10

OVERALL ATTITUDE TOWARDS OTHERS   0 1 2 3 4 5 6 7 8 9 10

_____   0 1 2 3 4 5 6 7 8 9 10

TODAY'S PRIORITIES

> " Comparison is the thief of joy. "

ONE WIN I HAD YESTERDAY WAS...

Things I'm thankful for:

1. _____

2. _____

3. _____

Today, I'm looking forward to:

Thoughts & Dreams

EVENING REFLECTION: Evaluate how content you are with these areas of your life today

HEALTH (CIRCLE FOR NUTRITION. MARK "X" FOR EXERCISE.)   0 1 2 3 4 5 6 7 8 9 10

OVERALL ATTITUDE TOWARDS MYSELF   0 1 2 3 4 5 6 7 8 9 10

OVERALL ATTITUDE TOWARDS OTHERS   0 1 2 3 4 5 6 7 8 9 10

_____   0 1 2 3 4 5 6 7 8 9 10

TODAY'S PRIORITIES

> Being an adult is like folding a fitted sheet. No one really knows how. Just keep doing your best.

Things I'm thankful for:

1. _____

2. _____

3. _____

ONE WIN I HAD YESTERDAY WAS...

Today, I'm looking forward to:

Thoughts & Dreams

EVENING REFLECTION: Evaluate how content you are with these areas of your life today

HEALTH (CIRCLE FOR NUTRITION. MARK "X" FOR EXERCISE.)   0 1 2 3 4 5 6 7 8 9 10

OVERALL ATTITUDE TOWARDS MYSELF   0 1 2 3 4 5 6 7 8 9 10

OVERALL ATTITUDE TOWARDS OTHERS   0 1 2 3 4 5 6 7 8 9 10

_____   0 1 2 3 4 5 6 7 8 9 10

TODAY'S PRIORITIES

> Many people will walk in and out of your life, but only true friends will leave footprints in your heart.
> -Eleanor Roosevelt

ONE WIN I HAD YESTERDAY WAS...

Things I'm thankful for:

1. _____
2. _____
3. _____

Today, I'm looking forward to:

Thoughts & Dreams

EVENING REFLECTION: Evaluate how content you are with these areas of your life today

HEALTH (CIRCLE FOR NUTRITION. MARK "X" FOR EXERCISE.)   0 1 2 3 4 5 6 7 8 9 10

OVERALL ATTITUDE TOWARDS MYSELF   0 1 2 3 4 5 6 7 8 9 10

OVERALL ATTITUDE TOWARDS OTHERS   0 1 2 3 4 5 6 7 8 9 10

_____   0 1 2 3 4 5 6 7 8 9 10

[TODAY'S PRIORITIES]

> " In the end, it's not the years in your life that count. It's the life in your years.
> -Abraham Lincoln "

Things I'm thankful for:

1. _____

2. _____

3. _____

ONE WIN I HAD YESTERDAY WAS...

Today, I'm looking forward to:

Thoughts & Dreams

EVENING REFLECTION: Evaluate how content you are with these areas of your life today

HEALTH (CIRCLE FOR NUTRITION. MARK "X" FOR EXERCISE.)   0 1 2 3 4 5 6 7 8 9 10

OVERALL ATTITUDE TOWARDS MYSELF   0 1 2 3 4 5 6 7 8 9 10

OVERALL ATTITUDE TOWARDS OTHERS   0 1 2 3 4 5 6 7 8 9 10

_____   0 1 2 3 4 5 6 7 8 9 10

LIST SOME WORDS in THE SUNBEAMS THAT DESCRIBE ATTRIBUTES YOU LOVE ABOUT YOURSELF

TODAY'S PRIORITIES

> " The willingness to show up changes us, It makes us a little braver each time.
> -Brené Brown "

Things I'm thankful for:

1. _____

2. _____

3. _____

ONE WIN I HAD YESTERDAY WAS...

Today, I'm looking forward to:

Thoughts & Dreams

EVENING REFLECTION: Evaluate how content you are with these areas of your life today

HEALTH (CIRCLE FOR NUTRITION. MARK "X" FOR EXERCISE.)   0 1 2 3 4 5 6 7 8 9 10

OVERALL ATTITUDE TOWARDS MYSELF   0 1 2 3 4 5 6 7 8 9 10

OVERALL ATTITUDE TOWARDS OTHERS   0 1 2 3 4 5 6 7 8 9 10

_____   0 1 2 3 4 5 6 7 8 9 10

TODAY'S PRIORITIES

> We have to choose between what is right, and what is easy.
> -J. K. Rowling

ONE WIN I HAD YESTERDAY WAS...

Things I'm thankful for:

1. _____

2. _____

3. _____

Today. I'm looking forward to:

Thoughts & Dreams

EVENING REFLECTION: Evaluate how content you are with these areas of your life today

HEALTH (CIRCLE FOR NUTRITION. MARK "X" FOR EXERCISE.)   0 1 2 3 4 5 6 7 8 9 10

OVERALL ATTITUDE TOWARDS MYSELF   0 1 2 3 4 5 6 7 8 9 10

OVERALL ATTITUDE TOWARDS OTHERS   0 1 2 3 4 5 6 7 8 9 10

_____   0 1 2 3 4 5 6 7 8 9 10

_ _ / _ _ / _ _ _ _ **DATE**

[TODAY'S PRIORITIES]

> " Happiness is the best makeup.
> -Drew Barrymore "

Things I'm thankful for:

1. _____

2. _____

3. _____

ONE WIN I HAD YESTERDAY WAS...

Today, I'm looking forward to:

Thoughts & Dreams

EVENING REFLECTION: Evaluate how content you are with these areas of your life today

HEALTH (CIRCLE FOR NUTRITION. MARK "X" FOR EXERCISE.)   0 1 2 3 4 5 6 7 8 9 10

OVERALL ATTITUDE TOWARDS MYSELF   0 1 2 3 4 5 6 7 8 9 10

OVERALL ATTITUDE TOWARDS OTHERS   0 1 2 3 4 5 6 7 8 9 10

_____   0 1 2 3 4 5 6 7 8 9 10

[TODAY'S PRIORITIES]

> " If you think you are too small to make a difference, try sleeping with a mosquito.
> -Dalai Lama "

ONE WIN I HAD YESTERDAY WAS...

Things I'm thankful for:

1. _____

2. _____

3. _____

Today. I'm looking forward to:

Thoughts & Dreams

EVENING REFLECTION: Evaluate how content you are with these areas of your life today

HEALTH (CIRCLE FOR NUTRITION. MARK "X" FOR EXERCISE.)　0 1 2 3 4 5 6 7 8 9 10

OVERALL ATTITUDE TOWARDS MYSELF　0 1 2 3 4 5 6 7 8 9 10

OVERALL ATTITUDE TOWARDS OTHERS　0 1 2 3 4 5 6 7 8 9 10

_____　0 1 2 3 4 5 6 7 8 9 10

TODAY'S PRIORITIES

> "The best thing to hold onto in life is each other."
> -Audrey Hepburn

ONE WIN I HAD YESTERDAY WAS...

Things I'm thankful for:

1. _____

2. _____

3. _____

Today, I'm looking forward to:

Thoughts & Dreams

EVENING REFLECTION: Evaluate how content you are with these areas of your life today

HEALTH (CIRCLE FOR NUTRITION. MARK "X" FOR EXERCISE.)   0 1 2 3 4 5 6 7 8 9 10

OVERALL ATTITUDE TOWARDS MYSELF   0 1 2 3 4 5 6 7 8 9 10

OVERALL ATTITUDE TOWARDS OTHERS   0 1 2 3 4 5 6 7 8 9 10

_____   0 1 2 3 4 5 6 7 8 9 10

TODAY'S PRIORITIES

> "Life's most persistent and urgent question is, 'What are you doing for others?
> -Martin Luther King, Jr."

Things I'm thankful for:

1. _____
2. _____
3. _____

ONE WIN I HAD YESTERDAY WAS...

Today, I'm looking forward to:

Thoughts & Dreams

EVENING REFLECTION: Evaluate how content you are with these areas of your life today

HEALTH (CIRCLE FOR NUTRITION. MARK "X" FOR EXERCISE.) 0 1 2 3 4 5 6 7 8 9 10

OVERALL ATTITUDE TOWARDS MYSELF 0 1 2 3 4 5 6 7 8 9 10

OVERALL ATTITUDE TOWARDS OTHERS 0 1 2 3 4 5 6 7 8 9 10

_____ 0 1 2 3 4 5 6 7 8 9 10

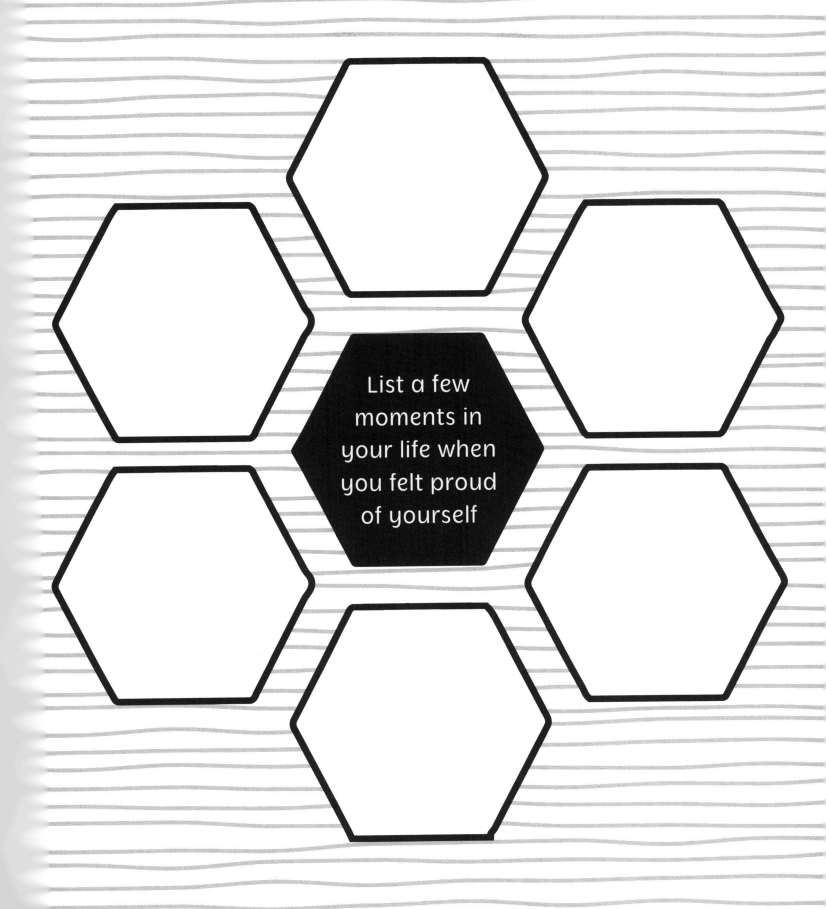

List a few moments in your life when you felt proud of yourself

TODAY'S PRIORITIES

———/———/———
DATE

" Today I will not stress over things I can't control. "

Things I'm thankful for:

1. _____

2. _____

3. _____

ONE WIN I HAD YESTERDAY WAS...

Today, I'm looking forward to:

Thoughts & Dreams

EVENING REFLECTION: Evaluate how content you are with these areas of your life today

HEALTH (CIRCLE FOR NUTRITION. MARK "X" FOR EXERCISE.) 0 1 2 3 4 5 6 7 8 9 10

OVERALL ATTITUDE TOWARDS MYSELF 0 1 2 3 4 5 6 7 8 9 10

OVERALL ATTITUDE TOWARDS OTHERS 0 1 2 3 4 5 6 7 8 9 10

_____ 0 1 2 3 4 5 6 7 8 9 10

TODAY'S PRIORITIES

> Stay close to people who feel like sunshine.

Things I'm thankful for:

1. _____
2. _____
3. _____

ONE WIN I HAD YESTERDAY WAS...

Today, I'm looking forward to:

Thoughts & Dreams

EVENING REFLECTION: Evaluate how content you are with these areas of your life today

HEALTH (CIRCLE FOR NUTRITION. MARK "X" FOR EXERCISE.) 0 1 2 3 4 5 6 7 8 9 10

OVERALL ATTITUDE TOWARDS MYSELF 0 1 2 3 4 5 6 7 8 9 10

OVERALL ATTITUDE TOWARDS OTHERS 0 1 2 3 4 5 6 7 8 9 10

_____ 0 1 2 3 4 5 6 7 8 9 10

TODAY'S PRIORITIES

> "If you don't like the road you're walking, start paving another one.
> -Dolly Parton"

ONE WIN I HAD YESTERDAY WAS...

Things I'm thankful for:

1. _____

2. _____

3. _____

Today, I'm looking forward to:

Thoughts & Dreams

EVENING REFLECTION: Evaluate how content you are with these areas of your life today

HEALTH (CIRCLE FOR NUTRITION. MARK "X" FOR EXERCISE.)   0 1 2 3 4 5 6 7 8 9 10

OVERALL ATTITUDE TOWARDS MYSELF   0 1 2 3 4 5 6 7 8 9 10

OVERALL ATTITUDE TOWARDS OTHERS   0 1 2 3 4 5 6 7 8 9 10

_____   0 1 2 3 4 5 6 7 8 9 10

No Season is Ever Wasted

◆ Cut out to display or frame for encouragement ◆

Enjoy the little things,
for one day
you'll look back
and realize
they were the big things.

Discover more titles from Creative Ideas Publishing

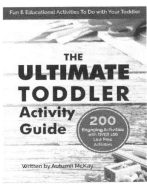